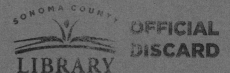

The Shell Book

Barbara Hirsch Lember

Houghton Mifflin Company
Boston

*The photographs were taken with black-and-white infrared
film and hand-tinted; they are reproduced in full color.*

My sincere gratitude to Elaine McDonald, a member of the Philadelphia Shell Club based at The Academy of Natural Sciences, for her kindness and generosity in lending me both research books and shells from her collection; with appreciation to Dr. Gary Rosenberg from The Academy of Natural Sciences for graciously spending time with me to verify shells and facts; thanks, also, to my husband, family, and friends—some of whom also lent me shells and background materials—for all their wonderful support; and to my editor Margaret Raymo and to my art director David Saylor: a big thank you for your trust and the ease with which we worked together.

Book design by David Saylor. The text of this book is set in 16-point Stempel Garamond.

Library of Congress Cataloging-in-Publication Data Lember, Barbara Hirsch. The shell book / by Barbara Hirsch Lember. p. cm. Summary: Describes a wide variety of shells, including the lion's paw, giant Atlantic cockle, and Katharine's chiton. ISBN 0-395-72030-3 1. Shells — Juvenile literature. 2. Mollusks — Juvenile literature. [1. Shells. 2. Mollusks.] I. Title. QL405.2.L45 1997 594'.0471 — dc20 96-22172 CIP AC

Manufactured in Singapore
TWP 10 9 8 7 6 5 4 3

For my mother, father, and sister
with fond memories of my childhood summers at the seashore

Shark Eye Moon Snail

This shell, prized by many who find them on the beaches, is from the family Naticidae. The Moon Snails are common along the east coast of the United States, but can also be found in nearly all parts of the world. This snail spends a great deal of time searching for small clams and snails in the sand. It then is able to drill a hole through the shell and rasp out the meat. You can also find their egg cases on the beaches. These are made with fine sand and are collar-shaped.   2¼ inches

Chestnut Cowrie

∽ The Cowrie Shell, which belongs to the Cypraeidae family, has been found in Africa, India, China, Europe, and in the Americas. Prized all over the world throughout history, they've been used as currency, ornaments, and religious symbols. Cowries have been found in ancient Indian graves in Canada and the United States. Most of the two hundred living species dwell in tropical waters and, unlike other shell species, they lay their eggs and sit on them. The Chestnut Cowrie is easily found along the beaches of the California coast.   1¾ inches

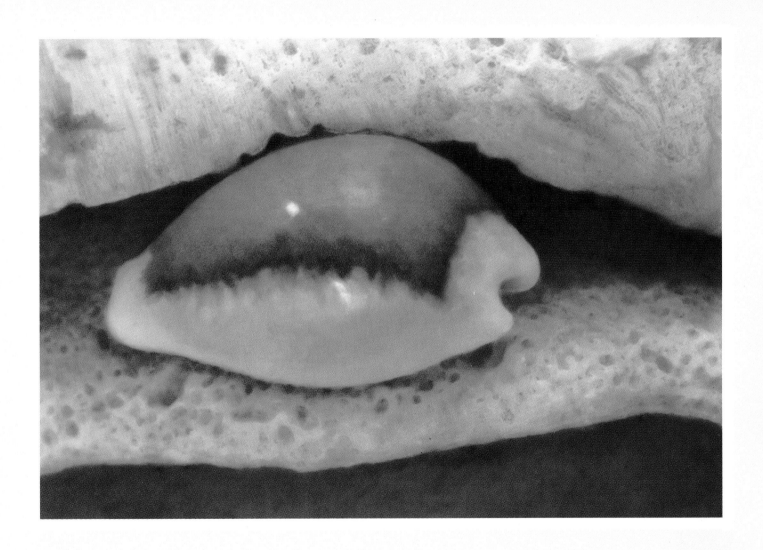

Giant Keyhole Limpet

∾ This shell is part of the Fissurellidae family. It is a common shell found on the West Coast from California to Mexico. Other kinds of limpets thrive throughout the world. They live mainly in intertidal, shallow, and warm water areas, and can be found on rocks that are below the low tide mark. They cling to the rocks through the use of the very powerful suction ability of their foot. The natural hole on the top is used by the snail for excretions.

3½ inches

Fighting Conch

 The True Conch family, Strombidae, includes a wide range of differences among the shells. These mollusks can leap and tumble, propelling themselves quickly by using their strong foot. Another unusual trait is they eat together in large groups. Most members of this family have a notch in the shell near the end, called a stromboid notch. The Fighting Conch is found from North Carolina to Florida and Texas. When alive, its color is intense. After it dies and is tumbled about by the waves, the color fades, and it can appear white. 3½ inches

Lettered Olive

~ The wonderfully glossy olive shell is found in warm and tropical seas all over the world. They are common shells which live on sandy bottoms at the surf zone or just below it. Though there are many variations in the markings, all olives are the same shape. They feed on small clams which they find through their sense of smell. Long ago, the Lettered Olive was used by Native Americans to make necklaces. It is from the large family known as Olividae.

2¼ inches

13

Giant Atlantic Cockle

～ This bivalve is also called the Great Heart Cockle. When the two parts are held together and viewed from the side, they make a heart shape. It is the largest of the Florida cockles and is easily found along beaches from Virginia to Texas. Other species of cockles are located in many parts of the world. Enjoyed as a seafood in Europe and Asia, the cockle was made famous in the Irish folk song "Sweet Molly Malone." The family name for the Cockle is Cardiidae.   3½ inches

15

Katharine's Chiton

∽ This unique shell, pronounced "ky-tun," is from the family Mopaliidae. Known as the Coat-of-Mail Shell, it is made up of eight overlapping plates that are banded together at the edge by a muscular ring of tough tissue. Sometimes you can find an individual plate, shaped like a butterfly, on the beach. There are about six hundred varieties found worldwide. Chitons cling tightly to rocks and are extremely difficult to remove. 2¾ inches

17

Lion's Paw

The scallop is a large and popular family, both for shell collections and as food. A member of the Pectinidae family, this variety of scallop has the wonderful name Lion's Paw. This shell has both knobs and ribbing, which strengthen the shell and protect it from its enemies. The Lion's Paw can be found from the Carolinas to Texas, and in the West Indies. When disturbed, many species of scallops are capable of rapidly swimming away by opening and closing their valves. 3¾ inches

19

Lightning Whelk

∽ This shell, whose markings resemble lightning flashes, is found in the southeast United States. The family name is Melongenidae. It is a left-handed species, with the shell opening on the left side instead of the right. The young shell is richly colored, but as the shell ages, the color fades to a grayish white. The Lightning Whelk uses its foot and the edge of its shell to pry open clams and feed on the meat. Whelk egg cases, which look like a chain of flat tan colored circles and are filled with hundreds of baby whelks, can be found along the beach.   3½ inches

Blue Mussel

A member of the Mytilidae family, the mussel is found all over the world and is a popular food in America as well as overseas. The live mussels attach themselves in colonies, where they are usually covered with water. As the tide recedes, they become easily visible. You can find them around wharf pilings, submerged driftwood, and rocky shorelines. Mussels have the ability to attach themselves to these surfaces through the use of their byssal threads. These threads are strong and thin. Their shells can be found washed up on many beaches.   3¼ inches

23

Junonia Volute

The Volutes, from the family Volutidae, are beautifully shaped and patterned shells. Most live in shallow tropical waters, but some live in deep waters and a few can be found in the Arctic seas. The Junonia live off the southeast coast of the United States. They are gastropods and have the ability to crawl quite rapidly. After major storms they can be found washed up on the beach. Some are also brought to shore by shrimpers, who accidentally catch them in their nets. 3 inches

25

Regal Thorny Oyster

∾ Not related to the true oyster, the Thorny Oyster is a truly impressive visual treat. It belongs to the Spondylidae family. It is also called a Chrysanthemum shell. These shells come in a wide variety of color and forms. The two halves of this bivalve are joined together by a ball and socket joint. The Regal Thorny Oyster attaches to rocks, coral ledges, and submerged wrecks in deep water, and is found from the Gulf of California to Panama.   4 inches

27

Cabbage Murex

 ᖰ The Murex is an interesting-looking family of shells. They tend to be spiny. This large family, collectively called Muricidae, is found mostly in tropical waters around the world. They tend to hide among rocks or coral rubble and become almost invisible because their long spines are usually overgrown with grass and sea moss. Long ago, Phoenicians, Greeks, and Romans made a rich purple dye out of a yellowish fluid secreted by the snail when it was boiled and treated. This dye was used to color cloth worn by emperors and Roman senators. 2¾ inches

Japanese Abalone

Abalone, also called sea ears, are found mostly in shallow water in places such as the Mediterranean Sea, in the Orient, and along the west coast of the United States from Alaska to Mexico. The Japanese Abalone can be found in Alaska and northern California. Because of its beautiful iridescent interior, it is often used to make jewelry. The row of holes on the shell is used for expelling water. Abalone usually eat seaweed and marine algae. There are seventy species of abalone, all in the Haliotidae family.

3¼ inches

32